Step Into The Dark

Julie Stevens

To Lydia,

Enjoy the poems,

[signature]

First published 2023 by The Hedgehog Poetry Press

Published in the UK by
The Hedgehog Poetry Press
Coppack House, 5
Churchill Avenue
Clevedon
BS21 6QW

www.hedgehogpress.co.uk

ISBN: 978-1-913499-14-3

Copyright © Julie Stevens 2023

9 8 7 6 5 4 3 2 1

A CIP Catalogue record for this book is available from the British Library.

Contents

Let the Dark Stay.. 5

The Road Ahead.. 6

The Beast Outside.. 7

Insomnia.. 8

Only at Night... 9

I'd Run with You... 10

Stuck Inside.. 11

Left Behind... 12

Gremlin... 13

Just Me... 14

A Spring Appointment 15

Future Tides... 16

Wilting Flower... 17

Visitor... 18

Is That You?.. 19

No Escape 20

Chasing Rain.. 21

A Coat to Last... 22

Step into the Dark 23

Run Again... 24

Speed Kills 25

The Sky is Lower Today 26

Playing Dead 27

Without Hands.. 28

Running is a Prize... 29

Remember Me 30

Not Today.. 31

U-Turn 32

Stand Ready.. 33

The Unthinkable 34

LET THE DARK STAY

I will sit with the dark and let it have me
each breath is my offering to keep it here,
my body is a table so now it can feed
take every dead bone and wrestle it dry.
When the curtains close, let them stay shut
dampen all colour, I don't need the glare,
a hollow room may welcome this mind
I am here and I am holding the dark.
Both hands carry days now tangled and torn
those simple tasks that wouldn't lie still,
every cursed hour that dragged me under
they are here, hearing my rage.
Don't try and find me to untie these ropes
blurring the bite will only feed this pain,
keep the door closed to secure my fight
I am here and I am holding the dark.

THE ROAD AHEAD

They say the dead walk this road
every time the moon showers light
on steps caught in its glare.

A line of broken souls
breezing earth's warm crust,
before mounting the wind to the sky.

The chilled air catches memories:
sugar-coated, hardened, raw.
An eternal collection for the library of life.

We walk the same path
surging forwards with ambition,
never knowing when our steps will take flight.

THE BEAST OUTSIDE

The anxiety of night delivers
an unfamiliar howl,
crawling in through windows
circling the room,
the miracle of morning never
arrives on time.
I count my breaths
until I realize I'm alive,
then thank the day for letting me in.

I expect to see a fierce grey cloud
hanging in our street,
people wrapped in tattered clothes
their faces covered in grime.
The beast may be here,
but it all looks the same.
For now, I'll shield myself inside.

I'm sheltering fear,
but I won't hold its hand.

INSOMNIA

Night shakes hurt the most.
Firm hands strangle the life
out of sedate songs.

You're awake
breathing the curse of noise,
as dark sniggers.

The hours clang,
trees thump the ground,
damp air sharpens knives.

Prickly reminders have lodged in bones,
ill words wrestle sore blood.
A bead of mourning rolls under skin.

You lie on this rack,
hear every rotten dream;
words swoop like snatching gulls.

ONLY AT NIGHT

When I sleep it's gone,
sometimes.

I have a different make-up,
wear feet that skim the ground
and run to dreams I miss.

I climb galaxies of hope,
wrap them round my shoulders
and sail without ever holding on.

There's a light filling the air
I hear everyone is well,
I know there is no slow.

Under sheets I lie believing,
glide along the night
and rise with everything intact.

When I step on the carpet
the room always vanishes,
there's never a wing to guide me in.

I'D RUN WITH YOU

Your legs pound the waking air
carry your desperate needs,
kick me as I sit still

on this long road to recovery
my legs refused to walk, but
time hasn't fixed the brakes

I'm afraid. It sneers as it drags
you to the end. I know
because I'm already there,

wanting to taste those leaves,
feel the air comb through this loss,
run up a mountain, I can't even climb.

It's the worst wait
you coming home, reminds me
again, how these legs used to run.

I will love you from inside,
wrap lycra round my neck
and pull tight.

STUCK INSIDE

I used to catch the wind
and sail with every moment I could hold,
but now I sit stale,
waiting for days to ignite.

The route to fulfilment remains blocked.
Coned off in an unbearable hold
that even daylight can no longer lighten.
Outside my window a heavy stillness hangs.

The minutes are climbing desperate hours
to empty words that lie ahead,
trapped within these walls of steel
I find the time to wait.

LEFT BEHIND

You can almost taste the air
through a window,
as you search the day sailing by.

A car anxiously turns,
or a rider, too headstrong to wave.

Sometimes they walk past,
voices glued together,
never hearing my dull hello.

I'm behind this wall of glass
trying to reach a face
that knows I'm here.

It's as if time has frozen inside,
sucked the colour from each hour,
left me wishing I could take part.

I will swallow their laughter
until someone finds my door.

GREMLIN

There isn't one day
when I wished you weren't here.

Standing on feet
I'm just like them.
I see the sky, like they do,
colour the air, like they do,
but you're always in my way.

Inside,
wherever you feel at home,
constantly ringing the bell
to tell me you're here.
Posting trouble
into parts you want
to hurt next.

There are two me's.
One that sits quietly
in control
and the other
who always fires the canon.

My illness,
my gremlin,
it's time you left.

JUST ME

When I close my eyes
I'm just me.
No one stumbling through life
no one seeking the truth,
just me.
I'm not searching for an antidote
not looking for understanding,
I'm just me.

When I close my eyes
I follow myself running,
watch me dancing on stage and
jumping down the stairs.
I'm never tired, nor cross,
never feeling let down,
I'm just me.

When I close my eyes
I see myself,
I'm the person I want to be.

A SPRING APPOINTMENT

You stand there welcoming me,
your beaming smile
inspiring flowers to bloom.

I'm offered a bench to rest
and speak my worries.
Such patience,
like the dutiful parent
waiting on spirited children.

Here is a Spring morning
listening to my words,
answering calmly and precisely
before a change bursts in.

I'm nervously glancing up at birds
spiralling in the dimming light.
This is your time Doctor,
tell me what I don't want to hear.

I shake my head
in the thundering rain,
stamping out my frustration
in sodden pools,
before lifting my hood
over my stormy world.

FUTURE TIDES

Memories flood in with
waves, pounding reminders of
how young and energetic I was,
adventuring to dangerous seas.

They're calling me now to
stand up and notice the
change that's swept in.
Thrown me onto a beach of stony reminders,
rolling out the truth of where I am.
I can hear them drifting in and out
announcing their loss.

A girl who could once romp over uneven ground
unbalancing stones and still stand firm
is now here, regarding her past self,
left with a grief
that feeds the question,
what will future tides bring in?

WILTING FLOWER

She picks the flowers
as soon as they start to bloom.
I tell her they won't last.
We put them in water
they light up the room,
for one day, maybe two.
The stems then droop,
the petals rain down
creating a windowsill flower bed,
soon a shrivelled mess.
I'm a wilting flower
losing petals every moment,
hurting as I watch them fall.
My stem is drooping
searching for some hidden strength.
No water will steady me,
my tears nourish no part.
Will you pick me up too?

VISITOR

She says she can help me
when the world rushes by,
guard me from being swept
into their urgent storm.

She says the road to envy will
only tire me more,
set me on a dangerous path
to where bitter tongues
spill more slates of sorrow.

I ponder on the hold she's
got on me here.
This window won't open now.
Meddling hands have stolen my release,
left me sick in this furnished tomb.

She says the best journeys are taken
with eyes that can see a view,
a ticket bought so you won't miss
the thrill, of passing laughter, shrieks
and a love held tight.

I know she will stay and will
not leave my room,
baggage she's left does not stand so easy,
her ways in time may open kind doors
but I didn't invite her here.

IS THAT YOU?

I know you're there again, behind,
where hands never leave a mark,
where skulking never throws a sound,
there is just me, holding my breath.

I sensed you on my shoulder
watching the gleam of a knife,
but you disappeared. Only this same room
so cold. I checked. And again.

There, through a window, you drift past,
near my bed, you crouch, waiting,
in each room, you follow
always feeding this cruel fear.

You are ready to take aim, grapple from behind,
but they say you're not real.
You are ready to take aim, grapple from behind,
but they say you're not real.

Not one dark being with a pulse.
Not one mark clawed when entering.
Not one trail from nearing boots.

They could be wrong. I check. And again.

NO ESCAPE

They always take me to the darkest land
and fill my head with thoughts that hurt,

words bounce hard, bruising my insides
leaving heavy, swollen questions.

My daily battle with the fiends inside
always losing before I wake,

the nights so long, they crack me open
seizing sleep as it tries to unwind.

Days rummaging down worn paths
calling answers that won't stop running,

they take me to the tormented land
where only still minds find their way home.

CHASING RAIN

If I step outside
the wind will drag me this way and that,
clouds will roar and soak me in chasing rain,
the air will be shrieking my fear, shadowing each step.

If I step outside
my footsteps will point down a broken paving slab,
ears will locate the passers-by framed together,
legs will be weighed down by every question.

But if I stay inside
the wolves will chase me from room to room,
fear flies will find me and scavenge my stomach,
the thought tigers will cage me and lock the door.

My carefully crafted balance has been shaken
everything trapped in this anxious storm,
I'm frantically searching for my book of perfect choices,
my umbrella of peace needs opening.

A COAT TO LAST

When you unzipped me I slouched,
arched like ninety years had moulded me
into a wilted figure,
limping towards the final whistle.

You left no skeleton to anchor this body
no firm muscle to strengthen my walk,
just a bowl of pulp
festering in a bag of skin.

Measure these arms, these legs
and cut a coat that can't be unravelled.
Stitch imperishable thread into
fabric strong as life itself,

then I'll wear it proud,
seize every chance waiting and
refuse obstacles born to hurt.
A coat fastened with hope.

STEP INTO THE DARK

Let the sun cover us and warm our leave
keep the air safe from death's call,
guide us on this lonely road.
Our walk outside is shackled with fear
bells of peace no longer sound,
roads falling lower than a foot's touch.
Life drags us along
to taste this unknown war;
tepid steps building fire.

RUN AGAIN

For a minute you think you can run again,
feel the hand of a gust pushing you hard
finger nails digging in like there's no
apology to give. But the North wind
doesn't blow up my street.

It lies slumbering in the sharp gravel
of a road, watching the stillness of life
hang, like a breathless tongue.
Death arrives early here.

Or so it seems. The passing of time is
a stifled hurricane stealing youth, leaving
rusting scars all over a body that pleads to run.
For a minute you think you still can.

A mind rooted in crossing the line
will outrun every storm trampling its path,
but it can never blast the hands of care.
This street won't let you go.

SPEED KILLS

Rain hurtles sharp as it cuts to the ground
unites with waves as it wrestles the sea,
a charge of wind will ignite a calm sky
before a crazed plane dismantles its call.

A thunderbolt will blaze every stunned flight
terrified fleeing alarmed by the sky's reach,
a ray of light will always travel wild
stealing the dark from unsuspecting eyes.

My toes start to twitch as the speed sinks in
but a chase to lost days won't help me now,
the ache inside is a stark reminder
to not run away from who I am.

THE SKY IS LOWER TODAY

There's less air to breathe,
clouds are reaching arms
hauling me back.

I'm in a lake of stench:
thick, rising sludge,
wading backwards.

Tormented thoughts seep in,
drowning an aching desire
to leave a hint of light.

Today I've had enough
a valley of hurt,
jaded as a disappearing moon.

When I find my bed
I'll wrestle onboard and
hope sleep is kind.

PLAYING DEAD

The last time you saw me I was dead.
Clowning with ghosts, up to no good
in my head, where nothing goes wrong.

Not out there, sick and lonely
trying to make myself heard,
trying to switch on this damn light
clinging to the side.

The world that wants me is in here,
where the dead can live.

Not out there, sick and lonely
where eyes let me down,
where *you* let me down
never seeing past my smiles.

The world that wants me is in here,
where the dead can live.

The trees know I'm there
letting me lean on their posts,
the birds know I'm there
filling sadness with song.

The dead know I'm there
waiting to strangle your fun.

WITHOUT HANDS

I can see the end now.
A thin shadow laid on the path
signalling each step.

Time has changed.
Clock ticks are now weary,
but he's slowed down too.

always at my side,
holding me up.
The path seems to stretch further

every time I start to walk.
How his words swallow gravel
and lay the ground smooth.

I want to grab a hand
but these sticks are too hot;
metal rods burning the way.

A tap for freedom, a tap building a wall.
Comfort is having you there
beating back storms.

You carry me,
even though your hands are tied.

RUNNING IS A PRIZE

And just like that, I can run
as wild as that dog's
fuel scraping the sky.

Wind tipping the field,
feet sailing each gust,
thumping a dangerous dance forward.

Two sticks in hand
almost left my side,
that dog would be crazed by metal's flight.

The squelch of mud
moulding each foot,
a print that yelped to be framed.

The joy of landing never felt so good.

REMEMBER ME

Remember me when I walked by your side,
always setting the pace,
always breathing in life.

Remember me when I could beat you every time,
running to catch victory
proudly hogging the line.

Remember me when I tap danced your song,
feet moving so fast
blurring your sight.

Remember me when we hit the shops,
not enough hands
to carry our dreams.

It's another world I've stepped into now,
one that carries me
no shopping in sight.

A different tune I'm tapping today,
steadying my feet
trying not to fall.

But the me inside
will forever be the same,
remember me.

NOT TODAY

Some days should come with a health warning,
carry you straight back to bed and say
you're not ready yet.

When you step out too soon
you hit a wall and the clock stops ticking.
Days like these have already closed down.

Forget the agenda you're carrying around
the quiet mood you've balanced on your head,
it will start to wobble, find the full bin

and before long you're carrying washing
dropping sandcastles on the floor,
arms and legs in a tangled mess.

The soggy list, a bird's nest in your pocket,
the specks of claret rain splattering a white top,
your day is running now.

Close the door and turn off the alarm,
freeze the night sky and drain the light,
tomorrow is asking for you.

U-TURN

Days can lead to sharp places
where each step scrapes the rising
blade of troubles.

Moments that set the hour on fire
hunting feelings and throwing them
to heartless flames.

They always take me when I
least expect, journey into grief,
rotting behind a content mind.

I will gather the storms and throw them
down the river of hurt,
no callous air will ruin my day.

STAND READY

(after Walt Whitman)

And if the body were empty
could it be stacked with bricks
underneath, holding you up,
but if the body were a wall,
would it ever carry you forwards?

And if the body were only water
would it stop running,
ripple a moment of unease,
or surge to the edge of a promise?

Because what makes the body hold on,
be fuelled with a force that knows to stand ready?

I suspect in every day there is a whisper:
in the silk of young skin,
a sound still nuzzling inside.

If a body stands open, it will know it's there.

THE UNTHINKABLE

Walk me to a field
with a rope to the sky,
show me how to climb
but don't question why.

Rest me on a beach
with shells rising from the sea,
show me how they pirouette
whilst balancing on a breeze.

Guard me in a storm
with clouds that never land,
show me how to hold
their wisdom in one hand.

Take me to a mountain
with one leap to its crown,
show me why they fear
being near the touch of ground.

Walk me to my home
whisper your last goodbye,
I'll show how you've given me wings
but don't question why.

ACKNOWLEDGMENTS

Thank you to the editors of the following publications in which some of these poems have appeared:

Ink Sweat & Tears (Insomnia, Pick of the Month, Oct 2021), The Honest Ulsterman, Acropolis Journal, The Poetry Kit, The Dawntreader (Indigo Dreams Publishing), Dear Reader, Crow of Minerva, Dodging the Rain, Impspired, Brian Moses' blog, Buzgaga, Ariel Chart, Lothlorien Poetry Journal, Inspiration in Isolation, Heron Clan VIII and IX, Fevers of the Mind, The Hedgehog Poetry Press, Icefloe Press, Boats Against the Current, Flights e-Journal, Black Nore Review and Dreich.

Huge thanks to my family, friends and medical personnel who have been a constant support.

Thank you to Steve Logan, Anna Saunders, Cambridge Stanza, The Bridge Poets, St Ives and The Commemoration Hall poetry group, Huntingdon who have given incredible mentoring, guidance and feedback on these poems. To Niche Comics Bookshop, Huntingdon for your wonderful support.

To Anna Saunders, Anne McMaster, Damien Donnelly and Steve Logan for spending their precious time with this book and writing such thoughtful comments.

I'd like to give particular thanks to Mark Davidson, editor of The Hedgehog Poetry Press, for believing in these poems.